SHARP STARS

WINNER, 2009 ISABELLA GARDNER POETRY AWARD

SHARP STARS

POEMS BY
SHARON BRYAN

AMERICAN POETS CONTINUUM SERIES, NO. 119

BOA EDITIONS, LTD. ※ ROCHESTER, NY ※ 2009

First Edition

For information about permission to reuse any material from this book please contact
The Permissions Company at www.permissionscompany.com or e-mail permdude@
eclipse.net.

Publications by BOA Editions, Ltd.—a not-for-profit corporation under section 501 (c) (3)
of the United States Internal Revenue Code—are made possible with funds from a variety
of sources, including public funds from the New York State Council on the Arts, a state
agency; the Literature Program of the National Endowment for the Arts; the County of
Monroe, NY; the Lannan Foundation for support of the Lannan Translations Selection
Series; the Sonia Raiziss Giop Charitable Foundation; the Mary S. Mulligan Charitable
Trust; the Rochester Area Community Foundation; the Arts & Cultural Council for
Greater Rochester; the Steeple-Jack Fund; the Ames-Amzalak Memorial Trust in memory
of Henry Ames, Semon Amzalak and Dan Amzalak; and contributions from many indi-
viduals nationwide.

See Colophon on page 104 for special individual acknowledgments.

Cover Design: Sandy Knight
Cover Art: "Joy Sparks of the Gods" by Hans Hofmann
Interior Design and Composition: Richard Foerster
Manufacturing: Lightning Source
BOA Logo: Mirko

Library of Congress Cataloging-in-Publication Data

Bryan, Sharon.
Sharp stars / Sharon Bryan. — 1st ed.
    p. cm. — (American poets continuum ; 119)
ISBN 978-1-934414-28-6
I. Title.
PS3552.R877S53 2009
811'.54—dc22

                              2009012653

NATIONAL
ENDOWMENT
FOR THE ARTS
A great nation
deserves great art.

BOA Editions, Ltd.
A. Poulin, Jr., Founder (1938–1996)
250 North Goodman Street, Suite 306
Rochester, NY 14607
www.boaeditions.org

State of the Arts

NYSCA

Contents

You can get wrecked in this dance.
—Bob Dylan, "Nettie Moore," from *Modern Times*

I

Big Band Theory

It all began with music,
with that much desire to be

in motion, waves of longing
with Nothing to pass through,

the pulsing you feel before
you hear it. The darkness couldn't

keep still, it began to sway,
then there were little flashes

of light, glints of brass
over the rumbling percussion,

the reeds began to weep and sing,
and suddenly the horns

tore bigger holes in the darkness—
we could finally see

where the music was coming from:
ordinary men in bow ties and black

jackets. But by then we had already
danced most of the night away.

Saying Things

Adam was born
blind: he could hear
burbles, drips, trickles,

whirs and chirps, snorts,
snuffles, thuds and creaks,
he could hear a voice

muttering in his head,
it said *Open your mouth,*
let the words fly out, and

when he said *scarlet tanager*,
he saw a bright bird,
when he said *pine tree*,

the bird landed on a branch,
he said *grassy bank*, and sat
down himself, *clear stream*,

and drank, he said *sun*, that was
almost too much light, *moon*,
that was better, he was beginning

to get the hang of this, *stars*
were so far away they made him
lonely, *Cassiopeia*, he said,

and they came a little closer—
Well, well, well, and three
deep holes appeared, brimming

with water, then he couldn't
resist, he said *hot damn, holy shit,*
what the hell is going on?

and the voice in his head said
Wash your mouth out
with soap—a lathered bar

slipped from his hand and
slid across the floor, *What*
we need, the voice said,

is a woman around the house,
and there she was in the window,
setting something on the sill—

Adam, honey, you must be hungry,
this apple pie will be cool soon...
and he followed his nose home.

What Adam came to like best
was lying with the woman
in the dark, it took him

back to his earliest memories,
before he could hear himself
think, before all the razzle-dazzle.

Bass Bass

Stringed fish thub
thub thubbing its way

downstream or wave-
grained instrument—

the words make a little
sizzle in my brain,

which twin is it, does it
rhyme with *ace* or *ass*,

my tongue trips over
itself when I come to

either one, am I at
the opera, jazz club,

bait shop, is something
keeping time or sifting it

through gills—you've
got the picture, here's

the quiz: *striped bass,
stringed bass, sea bass*

double bass, basswood—
what a difference a vowel

makes, this is the danger
you face, telling the story

of your life, if you fail
to enunciate perfectly

you could have yourself
all wrong, Bayzil not Basil,

married to Lisa not Liza,
writing for *Poultry* magazine—

how many close calls our
lives are made of—did

the palm reader say
You will have a long life

or *the wrong wife?*
Suppose god has bad hand-

writing or a lisp, and we've
misunderstood the messages:

In the begonia was the worm...
we mistook gardening advice

for the story of our lives—
god made lime, and separated

the lime from the bark, planted
seeds, they were fruitful and

vegetable, he looked at what he had
made and saw that it was food,

he was pleased, this was just
his first try, blessed were the leeks,

unheard of on earth until he
grew them, and the peas also,

he tasted them and found
that they were good, a god

could spend his life like that,
puttering in the garden, not

a care in the world beyond
watering his plants, growing

the sweetest, fattest tomatoes
in the universe—if only

he hadn't wanted to take a day
off to go fishing, so he created

fish and fishing line, and got
to looking at the line, thinking

what else it might be good for,
suppose he plucked it just like

that, and *that*, it sounded pretty
good, but by then he was tired,

he used almost the same names
for the stringed thing and the fish

that jerked hard on his line,
he got himself all tangled up

in words, until he didn't know
his bass from his treble,

he was in trouble, he saw
he needed help, so he invented

Mingus and other people
to show him which way was up.

Flood

You've won a trip for two,
all you have to do

is build the boat and say
goodbye to everyone

you know, knowing
they'll die as soon

as you're afloat, like
all the people on Krypton

once Superman was launched—
yet who wouldn't jump

at a chance to be saved,
especially when you can bring

all your favorite animals
and one other person

for company, what's a little
seasickness and buckets

of rain when you can land
on a freshly washed new

world with everything
you care about intact,

all you have to do is swallow
your contempt for a god

who blotted his copybook
and then asked you to help him

cover it up—and if you refuse
he'll just ask someone else

anyway, who might be less
deserving, less forgiving.

Why We Die

Someone spilled salt
or stepped on a crack,
someone left a window open

or looked back, a mistake
that small was all it took
to let death into the world—

which means we never had
a chance at immortality
like the one Circe offered

Odysseus, and he turned down
for no good reason—I want
a good reason life is dangled

in front of us for only
so many years and then
snuffed out, I know I could

appreciate beauty even if
it went on *forever*—lovely
word, the way it lingers

on the tongue—I might even
give up sex and go back
to being a single cell, to

multiplying by dividing,
if I could still feel the touch
of sun or wind or water against

a membrane, if I could sense
the difference between night
and day, if the little Mars

rover I lived in picked up
any signs of life, I don't even
believe in getting out of the way

of others clamoring in line
to try this ride, I just want
to stay right here watching

cows drink from a pond
on a moonlit night.
Because.

Charming Quarks

Here's the human brain
with its big bright eyes.
There's the universe

we live in, ninety-nine
percent dark—not exactly
a marriage made in heaven,

but an unfortunate mismatch,
Abelard and Blondie, or
Blondie in bifocals,

speculating… so maybe
if we were blind, or
the universe were visible,

we'd be in tune, on the same
wavelength—*all you have to do
is listen*, says one poet

of another's famously
quirky work—*all we have
to do is listen*, says Blondie,

*listen with our eyes closed,
and who knows what
secrets will be whispered*

*in the chambers of our
delicate ears? Just think
what blind fish must know,*

and bats, for that matter…
while she nattered on I began
to wonder if somewhere

there's a universe we were
made for, meant for, but
never happened to meet—

or maybe we knew it too well,
and left it for this mysterious
stranger—maybe it isn't gravity

that holds us here, but obsession
with whatever resists
our advances: Blondie puts on

a shorter skirt, Abelard
buys her one more book
on metaphysical love, and we

keep the lights burning,
look to the stars to guide
our lives, try to turn

a deaf ear to the darkness
that defines them and draws
us irresistibly toward it.

Stardust

If we are
        stardust, if flecks of it glitter
            in our bones,

is some part of the stars
        our dust? Do bits
            of the dead—the unwrapped,

unembalmed, unfettered
        dead, those free of the trappings
            of immortality—do they rise

seventeen times as high
        as the moon? Has a strand
            of someone's red hair

threaded its way through
        Saturn's rings? Is dark matter
            mottled, here and there,

with cells from a bright
        blue eye? Do infinitesimal sperm
            swim out of the Milky Way

and toward Andromeda? Suppose
        some fragment of consciousness
            managed to land on Mars—of course

it wouldn't matter, without a mouth,
        an ear, without a soul
            to tell its story to....

In the space museum
    each step down
        a two-story spiral walk

is 145 million years,
    from the beginning
        of the universe, past

the first stars, star clusters,
    other galaxies, eventually
        our own, and our own

solar system, at the edge
    of one curled—*arm*, we say, as if
        it cradled us,

we can't seem to help
    talking this way—
        and finally, at the end,

the present: on the ground
    floor, a human hair
        shows in scale

the span of human time
    on earth. Our little lives
        can't possibly be the point

of all this roiling
    fire and ice, any point there was
        shattered right at

the beginning, the universe
    unfolded without us—
        we're too small

even to be a mote
        in Orion's eye, and Orion,
                one of our supreme

fictions, is no more than a mote
        in the eyeless universe—
                I can't take it in, all this

meaninglessness on the one hand,
        and on the other our desperately
                meaningful lives—

as if the flickering of our comings
        and goings could hold
                a candle to the handwriting—

no, the mindless but beautifully
        formal scrawls—on the walls
                and ceiling.... What I think

right now is that mindlight
        casts a glow subtler, more
                nuanced than anything else

in the universe, for all its flash
        and glamor.... I held a baby
                once, in a hospital:

brain-damaged by meningitis
        and neglectful parents, it cried
                mechanically, tinnily,

nothing left but a brainstem,
        its flowering gone, and *that* sound
                is the real music of the universe

without us to make it matter—
    that's what I want to shout
        up the spiral staircase,

and I want my voice to carry
    out through the roof, past
        the moon and sun and stars

to the edge of space, the beginning
    of time, I want to say,
        We're coming, life is coming,

people are coming, words and music
    are coming, we will make something
        of you—but there is no *you.*

One of my teachers said
    Avoid personification, and I believe
        she was right: instead of seeing ourselves

wherever we look, we must see
    things for what they are:
        stardust. Soon enough

it will fill our lungs—
    as another teacher said, *So many*
        more ways to be dead than alive.

If value is based on scarcity,
    we're the most valuable things
        in the universe, even if

the universe doesn't know it.
    The most difficult part of writing
        a Shakespearean sonnet

is finding a two-line couplet
    that will somehow balance
        everything that's come

before it, but mere mortals
    set themselves this problem
        in the first place,

and have solved it
    over and over, in different
        ways—this form

is a part of the universe
    passing through us like a wave—
        a kind of kinship, a kind of love.

II

Bicycle

Babies follow the croon
of a single sentence before
they understand a word,

that's where we all start,
with a hum rising up
through our bodies and

spilling out our mouths,
so it isn't surprising
that someone proposed

this notion: let's take
aphasic patients, people
who hear but don't

understand what's said,
let's see what happens if
we set the words to music,

then they chose a woman
who couldn't do anything
on her own—the nurse

had to do it for her—and
the woman's family said
she loved "Bicycle Built

for Two." Sure enough, when
the nurse sang, a little sheepishly,
Nor-ma, Nor-ma, get up

and take your bath, we're all
waiting just to have lunch with you,
like magic Norma knew

her own name and everything else
she heard, music carried the words
in somehow, past the debris

in her brain, those sound waves
found her and floated her
out of her room, downstairs,

to the table, they took her
wherever she needed to go
for the rest of her days.

Glenn Gould Humming

If you don't want the sound
that could be coming

from any kid in headphones
accompanying your precious

Bach, call me and I'll come
to your house and collect

every record you own
that reminds you this divine

music was written and played
by mere mortals with sweaty

palms and opposable thumbs—
and you can forget about the man

you believe intrudes
on otherwise perfect preludes

and fugues.

White Space

There was no music
on the written page

before white space
intervened between

words and sentences,
lines and stanzas—

and words were grateful
because it sometimes

lifted and carried them
when they leaned

into it, and the better
they got to know it

the more they admired
its immaculate condition—

which made them feel
all spotty, so they hoped

if they rubbed elbows
with it long enough,

something of that purity
would rub off on them,

they began to aspire
to music's wordlessness,

since everything they did
was meant to point

to something beyond
themselves anyway—

maybe if they slowly dis-
appeared into the white space

no one would miss them,
they thought, in a fit

of longing and self-pity,
maybe they should retire

and leave the stage
to music's unblemished

perfection—but as they were
clambering down

they saw that without them
white space was nothing,

their part in things was
modest but crucial—to

hang around outside
the jazz joint that looks like

a hole in the wall, urging
passersby to stop and listen:

there isn't much to see, but
the music is really something.

Proust's Jukebox

He pushes B-16, Combray
    comes back to him,

C-19 the seaside, A-8
    the agony

of waiting in the dark for
    his mother's kiss—

he had the memories set
    to music

so he wouldn't have to stumble
    into them

as he did before, but could recall
    what he wanted when

he wanted by dropping a dime
    in the slot—

and even better, everything
    that didn't fit

the melody fell away, all
    the little bits

and pieces he could never make
    sense of, nothing's

left over, his life's become
    a musical,

an opera he can listen to
    from a distance,

it sounds a lot like someone
    else's song

he played one day by mistake:
    When they begin

the beguine... it brings back
    a memory

ever green... yes, yes,
    he thinks,

his English only so-so,
    one should always

begin at the beginning,
    just as he did,

Longtemps, je me suis couché
    de bonne heure....

For a long time I used to
    go to bed early....

The songwriter understands
    involuntary memory,

knows that desire requires
    the loved one's

absence—how could Marcel
    imagine Albertine

when she was in his arms,
    how could he see

Venice clearly until he was
    back in France?

And yet, who hasn't surrendered
    briefly, *Oh yes,*

let them begin the beguine,
    for a moment

the ideal haloes the real person
    in front of you...

and then the moment is lost,
    like all time,

and if you go looking for it,
    you never bring back

more than a few random scraps—
    the heat between

the two of you, the blister
    on your heel

from new patent leather shoes—
    all the rest

is invented: the grand romance
    or lost chance,

something to make the search
    worth it,

just the right setting for some
    tiny diamonds,

the perfect cup of tea for
    a few sweet crumbs.

Poetry

It's like tuning slowly
around our Zenith radio's
glowing shortwave dial

as I did as a child, listening
for voices from Madagascar,
Fiji, the Canary Islands,

I could spend hours like this,
eyes closed, ear pressed
to the speakers to catch

snatches of language
between high-pitched squeals
and long patches of static,

and though I can't understand
most of the words that do
come through, it's clear

what they say is urgent—
someone's in love, someone's
at war, no one's at peace—

so I do my best to get it down,
just in case I can see one day, how-
ever belatedly, what it all means.

The Poem

Sometimes I hear her first,
muttering and stumbling
through the underbrush,

sometimes she's sitting
in her favorite chair
before I know it, saying

nothing, hoping I won't
be able to stand the silence
between us, that I'll bend

her ear with all the news
and nonsense I've been dying
to pass on, and sometimes

I do, because who knows when
she'll be back, but other days
I'm feeling peckish or petulant

or just out of sorts or words or
steam, and at first she prods me
gently with questions, and when

that doesn't work, she tries
to put words in my mouth,
she coaxes and whines, she

wheedles, and if I can keep
my mouth shut long enough
she slams her pen down and

her notebook shut and stomps
off in a huff—and then I'm sorry
sorry sorry because now I won't

be able to sleep, with all I didn't
say swarming in my head,
and it's no comfort that she won't

be sleeping either, or will sleep
without dreaming of me or
anything else—the truth is

I don't know what I am
or what I want until
I hear myself say it to her.

Barking Dog

After an hour of trying to write
over the high-pitched yap coming
from a neighbor's yard, I decide
to let the dog into the poem,
hoping he'll be a charming detail
or at least curl up quietly
at my feet, but instead he pees
on the first three stanzas, and
though I see what he means,
I have no intention of taking
advice from a dog—he knows
nothing about the pleasures
of solitude, obviously, so what
can he know about poetry?
Johnny-one-note goes back
to barking, each yap's a first
draft he never revises, *just listen*,
I would tell him, if he spoke
my language, *listen and learn*,
but he goes on making the noise
I came in here—into the poem—
to get away from, the mindless
whine of everything that has no
words or music for its pain, and
the poem agrees with me, if we
can't teach this dog any new tricks
we want him out of here, out
of our hearing, out of the universe,
even, and a pox on his stupid,
cruel owner, an enemy of the arts.

Dragonfly

my eye
we called them
darning needles
and last night
when I dreamed
speedboat? small
plane? then felt
wings hum in my
upturned ear
I slapped myself
awake and tore
the intruder to
pieces, beyond
mending, before
it could stitch me
up in silence.

Bad Days

Such a clever species,
  Homo habilis, the toolmaker,
    making things the one thing

we've been consistently
  good at, but what were we
    thinking when we named

ourselves *Homo sapiens*,
  the wise ones? Maybe
    it was a little prayer

that failed—each day we add
  more poison to the soup
    we share, drain our bowls and

go back for more, as if we knew
  we'd taken a wrong turn somewhere
    and couldn't see any other way

out of the bind, the blind alley
  we're in, our place in the world,
    on the planet that hangs

like a jewel in photos taken
  from space: blue oceans, green
    continents, swirling white clouds—

there's a good chance we're looking
  at the only life in the universe,
    and on bad days I hope that

we're the most endangered
    species, that we'll exit, discreetly,
        stage right, while the party

is still in full swing—we aren't
    the hosts, after all, no one
        will miss us... How far back

would we have to go to unravel
    our mistake in the tapestry? Before
        the atom bomb? The automobile?

The wheel? Maybe we should have
    stayed in the forest, even if it meant
        no Shakespeare, no Bach, no Masaccio.

No Dickinson, Bishop, Szymborska.
    If art is our saving grace, then
        what I am I to make of Achilles'

shield bathed in blood, of men
    fiddled and fifed to their deaths
        on the battlefield, of concentration

camp orchestras playing to calm
    newcomers as they walked single-
        file to the smoking ovens—

music makes it easier to kill, easier to lie,
    easier to believe lies... So yes, I think,
        on bad days, take us back—before

the industrial revolution, before farming,
    before we lived in caves or spoke
        or discovered fire, lift us off

our feet and into the trees and leave us
there, harmlessly eating fruit, not even
poking anthills with bits of straw.

III

Sawdust

Why not lindendust,
    hackberry, hemlock,
live oak, maple, why
    name the remains
after the blade, not
    what it cut—

only now do I see
    that the air is full
of small sharp stars
    pinwheeling through
every living thing
    that gets in their way.

Body and Soul

They grow up together
but they aren't even fraternal

twins, they quarrel a lot
about where to go and what

to do, the body complains
about having to carry

the soul everywhere as if
it were some helpless cripple,

and the soul snipes that it can go
places the body never dreamed of,

then they quarrel over which one of them
does the dreaming, but the truth is

they can't live without each other and
they both know it, *anima, animosity,*

the diaphragm pumps like a bellows
and the soul pulls out all the stops—

sings at the top of its lungs, laughs
at its little jokes, it would like

to think it has the upper hand
and can leave whenever it wants—

but only as long as it knows
the door will be unlocked

when it sneaks back home before
the sun comes up, and when the body

says, *Where have you been?*, the soul
says, with a smirk, *I was at the end*

of my tether, and it was, like a diver
on the ocean floor or an astronaut

admiring the view from outside
the mother ship, and like them

it would be lost without its air
supply and protective clothing,

the body knows that and begins
to hum, *I get along without you*

very well, and the soul says, *Listen*
to that, you can't sing worth a lick

without me, they'll go on bickering
like this until death do them part—

and then, even if the soul seems
to float above the body for a moment,

like a flame above a candle, once
you pinch the wick it disappears.

Careless

The man who knew so much
suddenly doesn't know anything:

the poems he used to have
by heart, how to hold a pencil,

how to read, can't add two plus
two, couldn't tell you his shoe

size, let alone his favorite opera,
he wouldn't know the difference

between garlic and ginger
if you held them under his nose,

he's forgotten what his mother
taught him all those years ago,

before he went out the door:
his name, address, phone number,

a dime tucked in his pocket in case
he needed help—*don't lose it*—

but now he doesn't know
it's getting cold in here, doesn't

know someone's knocking and
calling the name he can't answer

to, doesn't know he forgot
to pick up his good blue suit

at the cleaners, the one everyone
will want him to wear—

what's to be done with him?
What's to be done with any of us—

wastrels, spendthrifts, squanderers?
Not one of us has learned—

after how many million chances?—
to hold on to what we have.

WPM, 1942–1997

Welling

Sorrow rises as if you
were the well, filling,

chills the stones, seeps
into the cracks between

them: how many people
would have to drink

from the little silver dipper
to carry your sorrow away?

My Last Night

I'll have friends over
if any friends are left.

My parents, I suppose,
will already be long gone.

I'll still have cats, of course—
I wonder who'll take them.

I hope it's the right time
of year for clementines'

little liquid moons: *Take, eat.*
I may not have a religious bone

in my body, as one friend said,
but I'm sorry I'll never see

my secular skeleton
once it's finally free

of me. For music: Gould's
Goldberg Variations—not the early

version, full of disbelief
in his own mortality,

and too exhausting anyway
for the old lady I hope to be—

but the one made late,
not long before he died,

where you can hear him hesitate
before he lets each note go.

Idyllic little scene, isn't it?
A quiet, elegant evening

before the hostess slips away—
no clanking machines, uniformed

strangers, harsh lights, no loss
of body fluids or dignity.

Would I like to sleep through
my own death? Is that possible?

Would my last dream reveal
what was coming? How would I know

what to make of it unless
I could tell someone after

the fact: *You'll never guess
what happened. Listen to this.*

The Underworld

When I lived in the foothills
birds flocked to the feeder:

house finches, goldfinches,
skyblue lazuli buntings,

impeccably dressed chickadees,
sparrows in work clothes, even

hummingbirds fastforwarding
through the trees. Some of them

disappeared after a week, headed
north, I thought, with the sun.

But the first cool day
they were back, then gone,

then back, more reliable
than weathermen, and I realized

they hadn't gone north at all,
but up the mountain, as invisible

to me as if they had flown
a thousand miles, yet in reality

just out of sight, out of reach—
maybe at the end of our lives

the world lifts that slightly
away from us, and returns once

or twice to see if we've refilled
the feeder, if we still remember it,

or if we've taken leave
of our senses altogether.

Afterlife

The Elysian fields unfold
their green carpets *here*,

inside me, all the way
to the horizon, the dead

stroll in the halflight,
sometimes muttering

to themselves or to me—
little fragments, a name

or place, an unfinished
thought, it's not conversation

but it's comforting to know
they're so close by—and I

begin to picture something
almost like a party,

old friends catching up,
introductions across

what would have been
centuries in life,

that's what I want
for them, and for myself

eventually, a dining car
full of interesting people,

steaming plates of food
set unobtrusively

at our elbows, and all
the while varied land-

scapes scrolling past
the windows—but in truth

I know the dead don't speak
to each other, only to me

or to you, or another one
of the living, they show up

unbidden, and I've never been
anything but glad to see them

or hear them, so I'd like
to think the feeling's

mutual, but if they feel
anything, it's loneliness

as they travel unfathomable
distances at the speed

of sound, the speed of light
to bury themselves in us—

who, despite our best
intentions, will become

their black holes, their
vanishing points.

Essential

Why does my tongue burn?
Why do my legs keep walking

after I lie down? Why
does my right hand tremble

midair? Burning-tongue
syndrome, restless-leg

syndrome, essential tremor:
this is what doctors say

when they don't know,
as if it were in my nature,

or my hand's nature,
to quiver like water

the perfect temperature
for poaching salmon—

maybe as someone said
about a great-great uncle's,

my right hand has *lost
its cunning*, no more

card tricks or other
sleight-of-hand (*slight*

not *slate*, I remind myself—
mispronouncing

is like dropping a stitch
in knitting, by the time

you notice it's become
a pattern, an accident's

become essential)—apparently
a slight unsteadiness comes

naturally to me, my body's way
of providing scalding reminders,

when my cup runneth over,
that I should go in awe

of the universe, more in awe
than in fear, that I should be

grateful for all that slips
so quickly through my fingers.

Erasures

My best lover ever
is dead. And

the second best.
Nothing to do

with me, it was years
since I'd seen them.

Still, they took
something with them

no one else knows
about me, and if I

know it, I know
only half, like every

other line of a poem.

Die Happy

What a shocking idea
or two: that anyone
could die happily, and

that this young woman
thinks I'm ready to be
such a person, how

old do I look to her,
I wonder, after I describe
something I've done

that pleased me, and she
says *You're lucky, now
you can die happy.* Good

grief, I think, I've barely
gotten started, I plan to live
to at least a hundred

and ten, and even then
I will not be going gentle
into any day or night—but

I like her, so I don't grab her
by the shoulders, look her
in the eyes and ask her if

that's what she believes
she'll do, when the time comes,
but she must, and I envy that

even more than I envy how little
attention she pays to the body
that carries her so quickly

everywhere she wants to go—
instead I watch her kneel to weed
my garden, the way she bends

down and jumps up without
thinking about it first or
afterwards, without making little

grunts and clicks—on second
thought, maybe she meant
she doesn't believe

she deserves that death *yet*,
even though she has a husband
and beautiful children, even though

she does this work of bringing
life out of the dead land, and rides
a yellow bicycle up and down

the hills—still, she must suppose
something important is left
undone, and that once she's

found it and done it, and so
made her life even happier,
she'll be willing to let it go—

what kind of logic is that?
Except that the alternative
is keeping your life unhappy

so you won't mind when
you feel it being tugged
out of your hands—finally

I hear my mistake, I've confused
an adverb with an adjective,
happily with *happy*, I've jumped—

despite my aching joints—
to the wrong conclusion, she didn't
mean she imagines me lying down

contentedly, flower clasped
in my hands, satisfied, but
that if I found myself—when

I find myself—suddenly going,
about to be gone, I'll be sorry
to say goodbye, but I won't be

filled with regret at what's left
undone, I won't have to check
stacks of baggage at the exit,

I will have spent myself well—
oh, what a wise woman
I hope she is, I hope there's a way

to love this life to distraction
without hating it for going on
without me, just as the daffodils

will, and Jane—when I was a child,
I thought the places we went
on vacation disappeared when we

went home, and some part of me
still wants to take the world
with me when I go—if I can't

have it, no one else can. But if Jane
can imagine it's possible to die
happy, surely someone who claims

to be a poet ought to be able
to do the same—just as yogis
try to die in a state of deepest

meditation—that's the grammar:
not that they try to die, or
are remotely glad to, but

that they hope to die rising
instead of falling, as if a dancer
disappeared at the top of her leap,

as if just before an avalanche
rolled over him, a young man
were caught in a friend's photo

wild with joy in mountain snow.

for Jane Peterson

Soup

We struggled without me,
says Charles Barkley

after a game he sat out,
as if he could be two

places at once, two
pronouns, grammar's

boundaries too flimsy
to contain his multifarious

identities—maybe he's been
reading Whitman, or

figured it out on his own:
whatever we are is too

slippery to get a grip on,
that's why we invented

pronouns and point of view,
not to name others but

to name the places our spirits
visit, constellations

of sympathy, empathy,
curiosity, *look what you*

can see from up here, or
over here... we meet

in the ether, wherever
it floats, and mingle there,

just as the metaphysicals
said, whether it's over

a meadow at dawn or
under a steaming stadium

roof: *we lost… we won,
we're number one*, even if

we never touched
the ball, just watched

from the sidelines—maybe
Barkley's been reading

his homophone, Bishop
Berkeley, and thinks

the game is all in our heads
anyway, so how much

does it matter who dunks
the ball and who can almost

feel it in his bones, who takes
real money to the bank and who

just imagines it burning a hole
in his pocket, since we're all

in this together, this human
soup we each want only

the best for—yet who of us
doesn't hope that when

we're no longer part of things,
a few will take a sip, smack

their lips, shake their heads,
and agree, even if they can't

quite name it, that something
subtle but essential is missing.

IV

Bluebird of Happiness

Once it was everywhere and ordinary,
I saw it all the time, or knew

where it was, nesting in clothesline poles
we were careful not to bang

when we hung our shirts and sheets
to dry, because we wanted it

to stay—and then I went away
and forgot it for years, and when

I remembered to ask, no one had seen it
anywhere, let alone right under

their noses, so it became one more
lost thing, and when friends heard

I was looking they called to say they'd seen it
at dawn or dusk, so I saw it too,

in my mind's eye—which didn't count,
this was about possession, I had to have it—

but in the meantime I came to love
the common finch and sparrow

squabbling at the feeder, all the birds
in plain sight right outside my window:

cardinals, flickers, juncos, redwing blackbirds,
hawks watching from treetops, even

a robin the first day of spring—or so I thought
until I picked up the binoculars, smiling

at the cliché, and discovered a bluebird
on the branch. And he stayed while I checked

to make sure it wasn't wishful thinking,
stayed until my wrists ached from holding

the glasses steady, until I started wanting
to get on with my life, but I was afraid

to look away from something rare, something
I might never see again—and then my mind

wandered and he was gone. I watched
the branch for a while, but there was no

bringing him back—he was a fact
of life, after all, not a figment

of my imagination. Nothing to do
but pick up my book and wait to learn

how my life had been changed by luck, and
a long, sweet look at the wordless world.

Ode Sentimentale

How could so much have
    depended

on a damned black and brown
    chicken

that appeared in our neighborhood
    one day,

flatfootedly blunt and unironic, pecking
    up bugs,

rubbing himself nests
    in the flowerbeds,

as eager for our company as for
    the chickenfeed

we went out and bought to keep him
    happy

with us—and he seemed to be:
    mornings

he waited on our porches for us
    to come out,

once he even posed on the rim of a rusted
    wheelbarrow

long enough to have his picture
    taken,

sometimes he ran across the yard
    toward me,

wings outstretched in greeting
    I hoped,

though he never let anyone get
    close enough

to touch him, still we took him to be
    a blessing

on us all, even after we found out he hadn't
    fallen

from the sky, but wandered off
    from a flock

two blocks away—he had chosen
    us,

so when his owner came up, peered over
    a fence

and said *Yup, he's mine*, then went home
    empty-handed,

we were pleased and relieved—even
    more so

when the chicken showed up again,
    bedraggled,

a day after we'd heard shrieking and barking
    and found nothing

but a pile of feathers under his favorite
    bush,

we congratulated him and each other
    on his survival,

he was obviously a lucky charm and charmed
    himself,

within a few days he celebrated
    by hopping

on a low fence and crowing
    all afternoon,

whoo-hoo, still here, cockadoodle
    doo,

as his black tailfeathers began
    to grow back

he strutted his stuff up and down
    the sidewalk,

even walked into the road to peer up
    at drivers

who stopped to shake their heads
    and smile—

one teenager who ordinarily wouldn't have
    spoken

to me asked, looking pleased
    with himself,

Why did *the chicken cross the road?*
    and waved

before he drove carefully around
    the dumb cluck—

so we began to talk about building the chicken
    a shelter

of some sort, a place where he could be
    safe

at night—but how would we build one
    the chicken

could go in and out of that wouldn't admit
    his enemies,

and how would he adjust, after living
    so long

as free as a bird—then one morning he was
    nowhere

in sight, and across a corner of my yard
    a swath

of feathers led from where he must have been
    nibbling

seedlings to the fence he almost made it
    under

before one of the local coyotes
    snapped

him up—it was clear he hadn't escaped
    this time,

but even so I searched up and down the street
    calling

Mis-ter Chick-en, Mis-ter Chick-en—we'd never
    come up with

a better name than that, almost as if we
    didn't want

to get too attached to what we knew
    was a passing

fancy, a fleeting grace note—
    most of all

a flesh and blood rooster more likely
    to die soon

than late under our benign
    neglect,

our careless love—this is the epitome
    of sentimentality,

feelings out of proportion to their
    object,

in this case weeping over a chicken
    I'd never touched,

let alone taken care of, one that peered up
    at me

and the cars he wandered in front of, first
    with one eye,

then the other, and seemed unable to
    add one

and one together to see my big-brained,
    dithering

species for what it is before he put his fragile
    life

if not in our hands than in our ken,
    our keeping.

Oh Boy

What were the Shakers
thinking, giving themselves

over to frenzied dancing,
letting themselves be shaken

by music, but never by sex—
that's what I'm asking myself

when Buddy Holly's song
shoots out of my stereo

speakers and lifts me
to my feet, elbows flapping,

shoulders shimmying, *All
my love, all my kissing,*

I remember what I've been
missing, this physical

abandon, the mind lulled
to a doze, nodding off like

all the heads of Cerberus,
no wonder our parents

thought rock and roll
was the open mouth of hell

waiting to swallow us whole,
but this is pure joy, this song,

oh boy, I am putty in its hands,
my bewildered cats watch

me get religion, I surrender
completely to His Hollyness—

something I couldn't quite do
in public as a teen, dying

to dance but paralyzed
by shyness until I finally

let myself go at a party
where no one knew

I was the girl who didn't
dance—my dictionary

is wrong, ecstasy doesn't
take me out of my body

but into it, I am not beside
myself, I have for glorious

minutes forgotten my cum-
bersome self in this divine

music, shed it like a suit
of clothes to step into these

waves breaking all around
me, just as the Shakers

must have, and maybe
they were right, maybe dancing

like this *is* as good as sex—
I am so many plucked strings,

His instrument, reduced
to sympathetic vibrations

that were the beginning
of everything, and if my end

is indeed in my beginning,
I swear if someone plays

this song after I am dead,
the ashes that were my body,

released at last from any self-
consciousness, will gather and

swirl and rise up in a whirl-
wind of thanks and farewell.

Eau de Vie

*I wanted to shout back at it, "maybe I didn't write you,
maybe I found you."*

—Hoagy Carmichael, on hearing "Stardust"
played for the first time

Nothing.

Something, but all alike. No-thing.

Small shifts, a little heavier
    here, lighter there, faint shadings:
    the beginning of this and that.

Lumps and clumps gathering
    into themselves. Generating
    heat. More heat. Firstlight.

Firstdark, specks of light.

Suns. A few of them circled
    by darker spots. One of these
    earth. Ten billion years
    had passed.

Hotter than hell: lightning, flaming
    volcanoes, unmitigated sun-
    shine.

Followed by a slow cooling off, calming
    down, gases rising, condensing, rain-
    water falling, the planet wrapped
    in atmosphere,

and in the seas, stirred by filtered
sunlight, little clusters and chains: amino
acids, RNA, DNA, eventually

packets of matter drawing
a line around themselves: cell
walls, the beginning of inside and out,
of life. Blue-green algae. Three
and a half billion years ago.

Sexual reproduction, coming together
and multiplying, not simply
dividing. The first kinds of life
that could die.

Multicelled organisms: sea pens, jellyfish.
The slow washing up of some forms
of life onto dry land, and plants
taking hold, learning to do
something new, use the light
for energy, no more waiting
for lightning to strike: chlorophyll
green. Less than a billion years
to go from there to

trees, and only another ninety
million for plants to flower. Some
produced berries: *Rubus idaeus*,
the red raspberry,

named for Mount Ida, where Trojans
picked and ate them around the time

of Jesus' birth, and nineteen hundred
and fifty-nine years later, I picked them

myself in Utah, four cents a cup, just enough,
if I were lucky,

to pay thirty dollars for my pepclub
uniform that fall...

we were up at four A.M, to be done
when noon sun

hit the field, and I couldn't imagine
how some people

did this for a living, not just pleasure
as the Trojans had,

presumably, and I would come home
to hot soup

and a bath and sleep all afternoon,
it's called *stoop labor*

because you do it on your knees,
as if you were taking

communion, and the sweet berries
I stole from myself

melted on my tongue. Even after
that summer, I still

loved raspberries, and must have told
the story to a man

who loved me, because one day he
brought home a bottle

of *framboise*, a perfectly clear elixir,
eau de vie, essence

of raspberry, it takes two pounds
of fruit to make

an ounce of liqueur, the fragile,
delicate berries

that have survived fire blight,
cane blight, crown

gall, fruit rot, root rot, powdery
mildew, the best

were crushed to pulp in a mill
somewhere in France—

this man's favorite country, maybe
because he'd been born

with its shape stained on his chest—
then the liquid

was heated until it evaporated up
a maze of chambers,

leaving behind pulp, seeds, any
small insects

that had been making their home
inside the tiny cups—

what rose up and crossed over
to the cooling chamber

was pure, and condensed into a liquid
clearer than water,

still the first siphonings
were discarded,

and the last, leaving just the *heart*
of the matter

to be bottled and shipped to America...
I was wary

because the liquid wasn't the red
I'd expected,

and even before the glass in his
outstretched hand

reached me, the fumes stung my eyes
and nose, and when

I bent my head it was like
inhaling fire,

I licked the rim to delay
taking a sip, but

finally tipped my head back and
swallowed—it flared

up the front of my skull, burned there,
nothing but heat, why

would someone who claimed
to love me

hand me this poison cup—
and then

the alcohol burned off and left
the flavor of

a thousand raspberries on
my stunned tongue,

and I understood I had indeed
received a gift

of love, distilled from rich earth
and what had been

drawn up from it, in that one taste
was the history

of the universe that had made it
possible, not left

behind but transformed, translated,
carried over

into those piercingly clear drops
I swallowed one

by one—as I listen to the notes
of what seems like

a simple melody gliding its way
down a scale, *Da-dah*

da-dah da-dah da-dah da-dah,
Hoagy hears it

clearly in his head, he's a genius
at plucking songs

out of the air—what must it
be like, that wordless

hearing that can only be sketched
out after the fact,

something that can never be put into
words, not even

when someone marks the path
with them:

And now the purple dusk of twilight
time…

I can tell you something of how
the universe

came to be, and the earth, raspberries,
framboise,

I could even tell you a little about
where love

came from, and more about where
it went, *But that*

was long ago… someone else
could tell you about

the sources of rhythm and
harmony, yet

absolutely nothing of how
a riffle of notes

clearer than framboise falls
wordlessly

into a composer's waiting ear,
and he picks it out

on the piano, and eventually
the rest of us,

mere mortals, can take con-
solation somehow

from these pure tones that drop
from the stars

into echoing wells at the very
center of our being.

At Last

At last, a reason
not to want to live

forever: the stars
are winking out,

apparently, although
it won't be apparent

to most of us any time
soon, one here,

one there, it will be
eons before noticeable

holes appear in Orion's
belt, for example, or

the Water-Bearer's
bucket, but just knowing

they're going out e-
ventually, who would

want to stay on
under what will become

an unpunctuated
sky, just a few faint grains

of light, not enough to make
anything of, nothing

to wish on, hitch
our wagons to, nothing

to lift us out of ourselves,
no pinpricks of hope

in our black box, no reason
to stay, no place to go.

Acknowledgments

Some of these poems have appeared in the following periodicals:

Alaska Quarterly: "Afterlife," "Bicycle";
The Iowa Review: "At Last," "Charming Quarks";
The Ohio Review: "Big Band Theory";
Poetry: "Body and Soul," "Saying Things";
Third Coast: "Careless," "My Last Night," "The Underworld";
TriQuarterly: "Oh Boy," "Stardust."

In addition to the family and friends who provided every kind of sustenance during the time these poems were written, I would like to thank Peggy Shumaker and Joe Usibelli, whose generosity gave me the space I needed to finish the book, and the Washington Arts Council for an Artist Trust Fellowship that gave me the time.

The Joy Sparks of the Gods, 1965, used with permission. © 2007 Estate of Hans Hofmann / Artists Rights Society (ARS), New York.

Quote from "Nettie Moore," written by Bob Dylan, reprinted with permission of Special Rider Music.

Quote from "Stardust": Music by HOAGY CARMICHAEL, Words by MITCHELL PARISH, French Translation by YVETTE BARUCH, © 1929 (Renewed) EMI MILLS MUSIC, INC. and HOAGY PUBLISHING COMPANY in the U.S. All Rights outside the U.S. Controlled by EMI MILLS MUSIC, INC. (Publishing) and ALFRED PUBLISHING CO., INC. (Print). All Rights Reserved. Used by Permission of ALFRED PUBLISHING CO., INC.

Quote from "Begin the Beguine": Words and Music by COLE PORTER, Spanish Version By MARIA GREVER, © 1935 (Renewed) WB MUSIC CORP. All Rights Administered by WB MUSIC CORP. (Publishing) and ALFRED PUBLISHING CO., INC. (Print). All Rights Reserved.

About the Author

Sharon Bryan is the author of three previous collections of poetry: *Salt Air* and *Objects of Affection* from Wesleyan University Press, and *Flying Blind* from Sarabande Books. She is also the editor of *Where We Stand: Women Poets on Literary Tradition*, published by Norton, and co-editor (with William Olsen) of *Planet on the Table: Poets on the Reading Life*, published by Sarabande. She received a BA in Philosophy, an MA in Physical Anthropology, and an MFA in Poetry. Her awards include two NEA Fellowships in Poetry, an Artist Trust grant from the Washington State Arts Council, and numerous other prizes and awards. She was poet-in-residence at The Frost Place in Franconia, New Hampshire, and a senior fellow at the Provincetown Artist Colony. Her poems have appeared in numerous magazines and anthologies. She has taught as a visiting poet at numerous universities, most recently the University of Connecticut.

BOA Editions, Ltd.
American Poets Continuum Series

Colophon

The Isabella Gardner Poetry Award is given biennially to a poet in mid-career with a new book of exceptional merit. Poet, actress, and associate editor of *Poetry* magazine, Isabella Gardner (1915–1981) published five celebrated collections of poetry, was three times nominated for the National Book Award, and was the first recipient of the New York State Walt Whitman Citation of Merit for Poetry. She championed the work of young and gifted poets, helping many of them to find publication.

The publication of this book is made possible, in part, by the special support of the following individuals:

Anonymous
Jeanne Marie Beaumont
Alan & Nancy Cameros
Bernadette Catalana
Gwen & Gary Conners
Susan DeWitt Davie
Peter & Suzanne Durant
Pete & Bev French
Judy & Dane Gordon
Kip & Debby Hale
Bob & Willy Hursh
Robin Hursh
Nora A. Jones
X. J. & Dorothy M. Kennedy

Laurie Kutchins
Rosemary & Lewis Lloyd
Peter & Phyllis Makuck
Juniper & Marlowe
Elissa & Ernie Orlando
Peter Pereira & Dean Allan
Boo Poulin
Deborah Ronnen & Sherman Levey
Steven O. Russell & Phyllis Rifkin-Russell
Vicki & Richard Schwartz
Kay Wallace
Pat & Mike Wilder
Glenn & Helen William